Read & Understand

ENGLISH COMPREHENSION

Shab

A BEGINNERS' SERIES

BOOK 1

AF798544

priority PUBLICATIONS

priority
PUBLICATIONS

Published by Priority Publications
info@dspublishers.com

11th Impression 2022

9788180221187

Printed & Bound by : Sanjeev Offset Printer, Delhi- 39

₹ 199

Contents

MY PET DOG

I have a dog at home. His name is Rocky. He is an intelligent dog. He wags his tail when he sees my father. He barks at strangers. I love my dog very much.

Rearrange the jumbled letters:

1) mena ____________
2) fehtar ____________
3) heom ____________
4) Ryokc ____________
5) rabks ____________
6) ryve ____________
7) inlteligten ____________
8) trsanrsge ____________

DOING ACTIONS - 1

Mary is **carrying** a basket in her hand.

Jane is **lighting** a candle.

Jack is **throwing** stones in the water.

Tara is **holding** her father's hand.

Lucy is **chopping** a carrot.

The baby is **drinking** milk.

Choose the correct word from the box and fill in the blanks:

holding	**carrying**
drinking	**lighting**
throwing	**chopping**

1) Jack is ____________ stones in the water.

2) Tara is ____________ her father's hand.

3) Mary is _________ a basket in her hand.

4) The baby is _______________ milk.

5) Jane is ____________ a candle.

6) Lucy is ____________ a carrot.

Circle the 'Proper Nouns':

1) Mary is carrying a basket.

2) Jack is throwing stones in the water.

3) Lucy is chopping a carrot.

4) Tara is holding her father's hand.

TWO LITTLE DICKY BIRDS

Two little dicky birds
Sat upon a wall;
One named Peter,
The other named Paul.

Fly away Peter!
Fly away Paul!
Come back Peter!
Come back Paul!

Strike out (✗) the incorrect option:

1) Two little dicky

a) hens b) birds

2) Sat upon a

a) tree b) wall

3) One named

a) Peter b) Robin

4) The other named

a) Jones b) Paul

Choose the correct letters and complete the words:

1) Litt__ (el, le, il)

2) __on (up, ap, op)

3) B__ds (er, ur, ir)

4) Oth__ (er, ar, re)

5) Pet__ (ar, er, re)

6) Di__y (kc, ck, kk)

7) Nam__ (de, ed, dd)

8) Aw__ (ey, ay, ya)

PARTS OF MY BODY

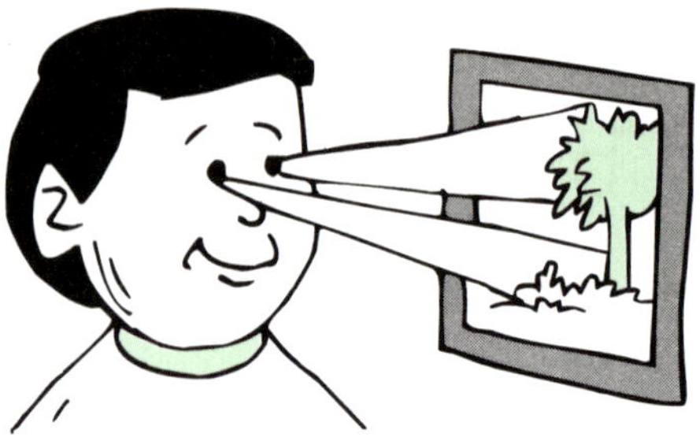

I see with my **eyes**.

I smell with my **nose**.

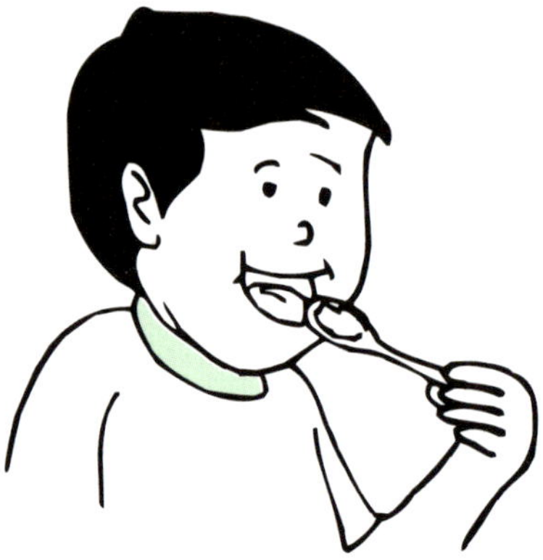

I eat with my **mouth**.

I clap with my **hands**.

I walk with my **legs**.

I hear with
my **ears**.

Write True (T) or False (F):

1) I walk with my hands. ( )
2) I eat with my mouth. ( )
3) I smell with my nose. ( )
4) I hear with my eyes. ( )
5) I clap with my ears. ( )
6) I see with my eyes. ( )

Rearrange the jumbled words and write the sentences correctly:

1) my I eat mouth with. ____________________
2) eyes my I see with. ____________________
3) with I walk legs my. ____________________
4) clap hands I my with. ____________________
5) my with hear I ears. ____________________

THE CUNNING JACKAL

One day, a crow was sitting on a tree, eating a piece of bread. A hungry jackal saw the bread and wanted to eat it. He went to the crow and said, "Your voice is very beautiful, O dear Crow! Please sing a song!" The crow was flattered. As soon as he opened his mouth to sing, the bread fell down. The cunning jackal quickly took the bread and ran away.

Fill in the blanks:

1) A crow was ____________ on a tree.

2) He was __________ a piece of bread.

3) A hungry ________ saw the bread and ___________ to eat it.

4) Your voice is very ____________.

5) The _________ was flattered.

6) He opened his __________ to sing.

7) The bread __________ down.

8) The jackal took the bread and ran ________.

MY DOLL

My mother gave me a pretty doll for my birthday. My doll's name is Lucy. She wears a beautiful frock. She has blue eyes and soft black hair. I play with Lucy. When I lay her down, she closes her eyes. When I sleep, she sleeps next to me. Lucy is my favourite doll.

Complete the sentences:

1) My mother gave me a ________ ________.

2) My doll's name is ________.

3) She wears a ____________ frock.

4) She has blue ____ and soft _____ hair.

5) When I lay her ______, she ______ her eyes.

6) When I ______, she sleeps _____ to me.

7) Lucy is my _____________ doll.

Circle the correct spelling:

1)	(a)	pritty	(b)	pretty
2)	(a)	birthday	(b)	berthday
3)	(a)	cloases	(b)	closes
4)	(a)	mother	(b)	mather
5)	(a)	favarite	(b)	favourite

GOOD HABITS

Wake up early.

Brush your teeth twice a day.

Take a bath every day.

Wear clean clothes.

Go to sleep early.

Show respect to elders.

Say "Sorry" when you do something wrong.

Say "Thank you" when you receive a gift.

Strike out (✗) the incorrect option:

1) Wake up

a) early b) late

2) Brush your teeth

a) twice a week b) twice a day

3) Go to sleep

a) late b) early

4) Show respect to

a) elders b) thieves

THE RABBIT AND ITS BABY

Once, a mother rabbit and her baby lived in a burrow. One morning, the mother told her son, "I'm going out to get some carrots. Stay at home. Do not go out!" When the mother rabbit left, her son slowly came out and began to hop around. Suddenly, he heard a tiger's growl. The little rabbit started to cry. When the mother rabbit heard her son's cry, she came

running and carried her baby home. The baby rabbit said, "Sorry, mother! I'll always listen to you. I will never go out alone."

Fill in the blanks:

1) The mother rabbit went out to get some ________ .

2) The baby rabbit heard a __________ growl.

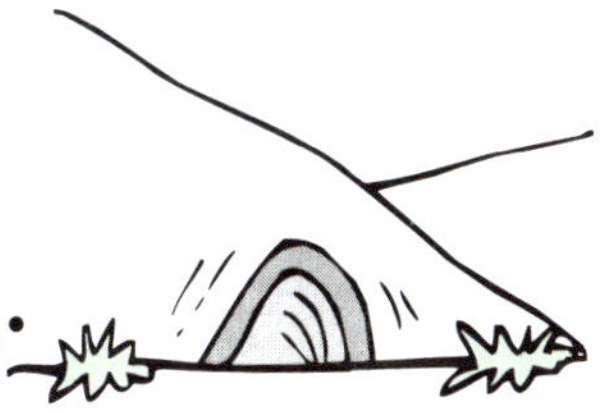

3) The rabbits lived in a _______.

4) The mother rabbit _________ her baby home.

5) When the mother rabbit left, her son slowly came ________.

6) The little rabbit started to ______.

WHO AM I ?

Tick (✓) the correct option:

I am very huge.
My ears are very big.
I have a trunk.

(a) Cow ☐ (b) Elephant ☐

(c) Dog ☐ (d) Cat ☐

I am beautiful.
I have seven colours.
You can see me in the sky.

(a) Clouds ☐ (b) Rainbow ☐

(c) Sun ☐ (d) Moon ☐

I am small.
I have a bushy tail.
I like carrots.

(a) Dog ☐ (b) Cat ☐

(c) Rabbit ☐ (d) Cow ☐

I have two colourful wings.
I sit on the flowers.
I drink honey.

(a) Ant ☐ (b) Crow ☐

(c) Butterfly ☐ (d) Grasshopper ☐

LITTLE JACK HORNER

Little Jack Horner
Sat in a corner,
Eating his
Christmas pie;

He put in his thumb,
And pulled out a plum,
And said,
"What a good boy am I!"

Choose the correct option and fill in the blanks:

1) Little Jack Horner
_________ in a corner.

sat | stood

2) Eating his Christmas _______.

cake | pie

3) He put in his _____________.

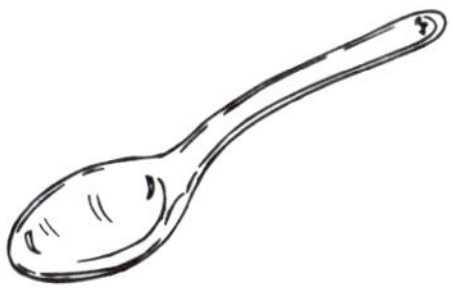 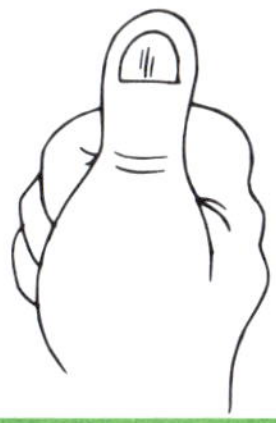

spoon | thumb

4) And pulled out a ____________.

apple | plum

5) What a good ____________ am I!

girl | boy

MY FATHER

My father is a doctor. Every morning, he goes to the hospital. He treats patients in the hospital. Nurses help my father. He is a very busy person. He comes back home only in the evening. I love my father very much. When I grow up, I want to become a doctor like him.

Colour the correct option:

1) My father is a......

Nurse

Doctor

2) ...... help my father.

Nurses

Friends

3) He comes home in the ......

Night

Evening

THE ELEPHANT

The elephant lives in the forest. Its body is very huge. It has wide, large ears and a long trunk. It drinks water with its trunk.

The elephant loves to eat tender bamboo and sugarcane. A group of elephants is called a herd. The baby elephant is called a calf.

Write True (T) or False (F):

1) An elephant is a small animal. ( )

2) The elephant eats sugarcane. ( )

3) Its ears are small. ( )

4) The baby elephant is called a calf. ( )

5) It eats food with its trunk. ( )

6) The elephant hates to eat tender bamboo. ( )

7) A group of elephants is called a herd. ( )

MY MOTHER

Every day, my mother takes me to school. She holds my hand while crossing the road. Sometimes, she buys me candy and ice-cream. She cooks tasty food for my family.

At the bedtime, my mother tells me nice stories. She also helps me in my studies. My mother loves me and I love her, too.

Choose the correct word from the box and fill in the blanks:

candy	**tasty food**
to school	**ice-cream**
nice stories	**studies**

1) My mother takes me ______________.
2) She cooks ______________.
3) My mother tells me ______________.
4) She helps me in my ______________.
5) She buys me __________ and __________.

Label the pictures choosing the words from the triangle:

storybooks
candies
food

____

____

____

THE DOVE AND THE ANT

A dove and a big red ant were very good friends. They always helped each other. One day, a hunter saw the dove sitting on a tree. He took his bow and arrow and aimed at the dove.

The ant saw the hunter. He ran fast and bit hard on the hunter's toe. The hunter cried loudly in pain. He dropped the arrow. The dove saw the hunter and flew away. He thanked the red ant for saving his life.

Fill in the blanks:

1) The __________ and the _________ were very good friends.

2) They always ______________ each other.

3) One day, a ____________ saw the dove.

4) The hunter cried loudly in _________.

5) The ant _______ hard on the hunter's toe.

6) The dove saw the hunter and flew ____.

7) He ______ the red ant for saving his life.

MY VISIT TO THE ZOO

Last Sunday, we went to the zoo. There were many animals in the zoo. We saw a lion, a monkey, a bear and a huge elephant.

I touched the elephant's trunk. We gave bananas to the monkeys. The lion and the bear were inside the cage. We enjoyed our day.

Write 'RIGHT' or 'WRONG' in the boxes:

1) Last Sunday, we went to the zoo. [ ]

2) There were no animals in the zoo. [ ]

3) We saw a lion, a monkey, a bear and a huge elephant. [ ]

4) I did not touch the elephant's trunk. [ ]

5) We pelted stones at the monkeys. [ ]

Choose the correct letters and complete the words:

1) l__t (es, os, as)

2) ga__ (ev, ve, se)

3) in__de (si, sy, ci)

4) en__yed (jo, to, po)

5) tr__k (an, un, en)

6) m__key (on, en, an)

MY BEST FRIEND

I have many friends but my best friend is Rita. She comes home on Sundays and we play games together. Sometimes, my mother takes us to the park. We like to sit on the swing. When the swing goes high in the air, we shout out loud.

Match the following:

1) Rita is	a) games together
2) We like to sit	b) to the park
3) She comes home	c) we shout out loud
4) My mother takes us	d) on Sundays
5) When the swing goes high	e) my best friend
6) I have	f) on the swing
7) We play	g) many friends

MY GARDEN

We have a beautiful garden at home. My mother waters the plants every day. The flowers bloom in the morning. I like to smell and touch the roses. Butterflies come and sit on the flowers. My sister and I play in the garden and watch the butterflies.

Write True (T) or False (F):

1) My uncle waters the plants. ( )

2) The flowers bloom in the evening. ( )

3) My sister and I play in the garden. ( )

4) I do not like to smell the roses. ( )

5) Butterflies sit on the flowers. ( )

6) My garden is not beautiful. ( )

7) We watch the butterflies. ( )

Rearrange the jumbled letters and write the words correctly:

1) ifulbeaut

____

2) mrningo

____

3) dengra

____

4) fowersl

____

5) terfliesbut

____

6) lantsp

____

MY BIRTHDAY

Yesterday was my birthday. My mother had baked a beautiful, big cake. She kept five candles on it. She had also made chocolate ice cream.

My father gave me a bicycle. All my friends came for my birthday! They sang the "Happy Birthday" song. We all played games and ate cake and ice cream.

Fill in the blanks:

1) All my ______________ came for my birthday.

2) My father gave me a ____________ .

3) My mother had ___________ a cake.

4) We all ____________ games.

5) My friends sang the _____________ song.

6) My mother ______________ five candles on the cake.

MATCH THEM UP

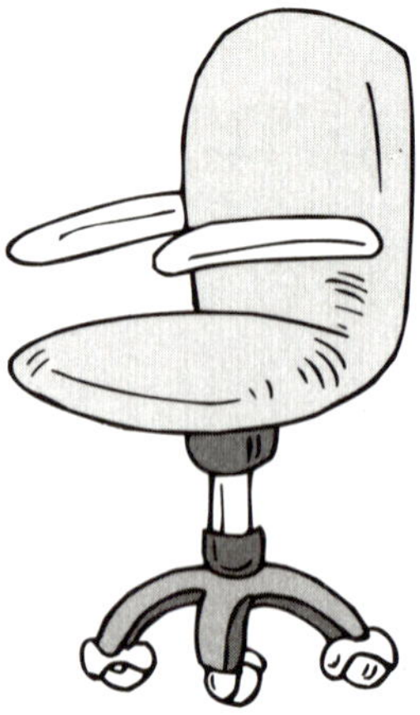

Doctor

Chair

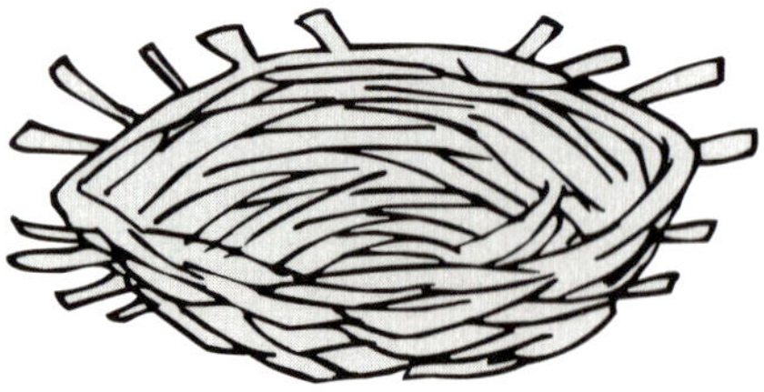

Nest

Nurse

Table

Bird

Teacher

Jam

Bread

Ball

Racket

Blackboard

Cow

Clouds

Rain

Milk

Choose the correct letter from the bracket to complete the word:

1) Br ___ ad (a, e, o)

2) Ne ___ t (s, t, r)

3) Rai ___ (p, n, s)

4) Nur___ e (r, s, i)

5) T ___ ble (b, a, e)

6) Clo ___ ds (p, u, s)

FRUITS

Orange

Pineapple

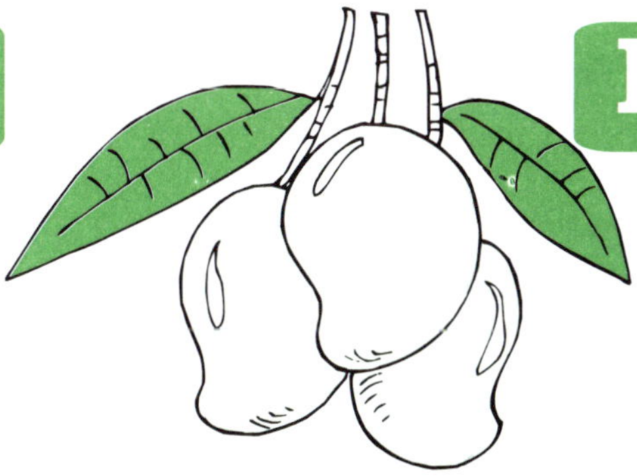

Mangoes

Bananas

Apple

Peach

Grapes

Pear

VEGETABLES

Tomato

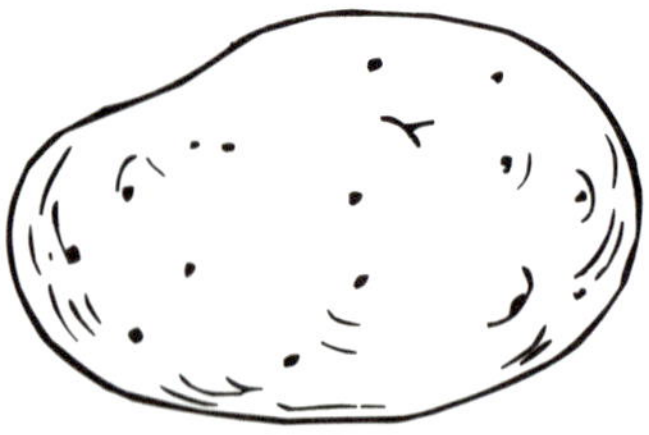

Potato

Carrot

Onion

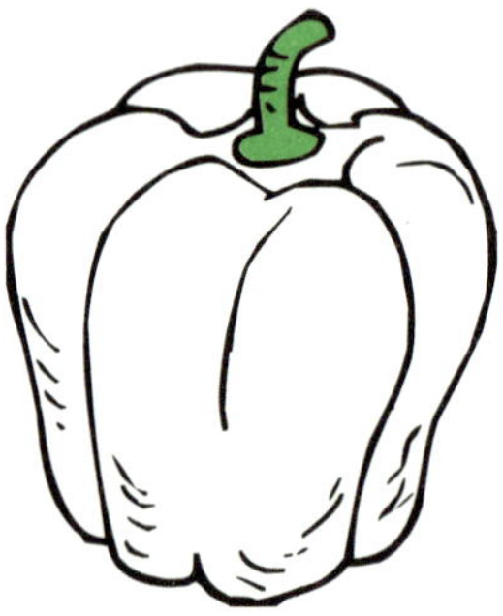

Capsicum

Cauliflower

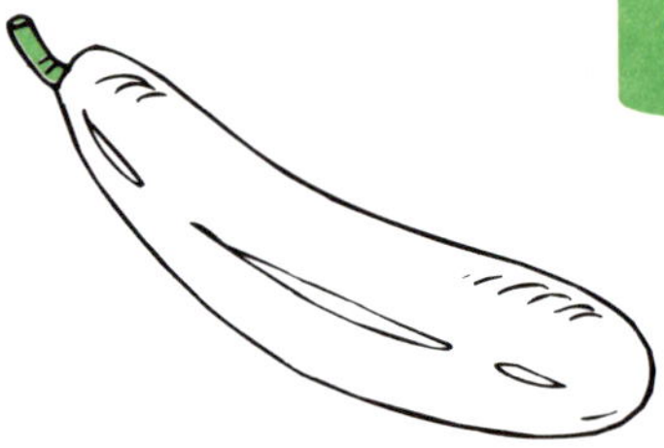

Cucumber

Radish

Pumpkin

Write True (T) or False (F):

1) Apple is a vegetable. ( )

2) Carrot is a fruit. ( )

3) Banana is a fruit. ( )

4) Mango is a vegetable. ( )

5) Orange is a fruit. ( )

6) Cabbage is a fruit. ( )

7) Peach is a fruit. ( )

8) Onion is a vegetable. ( )

MARY HAD A LITTLE LAMB

Mary had a little lamb
little lamb, little lamb
Mary had a little lamb
Its fleece was white as snow.

And everywhere that Mary went
Mary went, Mary went
Everywhere that Mary went
The lamb was sure to go.

Fill in the blanks:

1) Mary had a ____________ lamb.

2) It's _____________ was white as snow.

3) Everywhere that Mary ____________ .

4) The _______ was sure to _________ .

Match the following:

1) Everywhere that	a) to go
2) The fleece was	b) a little lamb
3) Mary had	c) Mary went
4) The lamb was sure	d) white as snow

SOUNDS OF ANIMALS

A dog barks.

A tiger growls.

A lion roars.

A wolf howls.

An elephant trumpets.

A cat mews.

Match the animals with the sounds:

1) An elephant	a) barks
2) A cat	b) roars
3) A lion	c) howls
4) A wolf	d) growls
5) A dog	e) trumpets
6) A tiger	f) mews

MY TOYS

My sister and I like to play with toys. My sister likes dolls. She has a good collection of beautiful dolls. I like cars. I have many cars of different models and colours.

My sister has got a doll which talks. I have got a car which goes very fast. My father brought it for me on my last birthday. Together, my sister and I have lot of fun with our toys.

Match the following:

1) My sister	a) talks
2) Her doll	b) goes fast
3) My car	c) likes dolls
4) I have	d) brought the car
5) My father	e) have lot of fun
6) My sister and I	f) many cars

Label the pictures choosing the words from the box:

____

____

My sister
My father
Doll
Car

____

____

BAA, BAA, BLACK SHEEP

Baa, baa, black sheep,
Have you any wool?
Yes sir! Yes sir!
Three bags full.

One for my master,
One for my dame,
And one for the little boy,
Who lives down the lane.

Arrange the sentences in the correct order:

1) Three bags full. ( )

2) Have you any wool? ( )

3) Baa, baa, black sheep, ( )

4) Yes sir! Yes sir! ( )

5) One for my master, ( )

6) Who lives down the lane. ( )

7) And One for the little boy, ( )

8) One for my dame, ( )

Match the pictures with the text:

1)

a) One for my
master,
one for my
dame.

2)

b) Baa, baa,
black sheep,
have you any
wool?

3)

c) And one for
the little boy,
who lives
down the lane.

4)

d) Yes sir!
Yes sir!
Three bags
full.

THE FOX AND THE GRAPES

One day, a hungry fox was wandering through the forest. Suddenly, he saw a vineyard, full of juicy grapes. The fox was delighted. "Ah, I shall have a delicious breakfast!" he thought, entering the vineyard. But, the grapes were hanging very high. The fox jumped up, trying to pluck the grapes, but in vain. No matter how hard the fox tried, he could not grab the grapes. At last, he gave up. To hide his

disappointment, he sneered, "Good that I could not eat those grapes. They look sour anyway." And so saying, the fox walked away.

Complete the paragraph:

One day, a ________  was wandering through the forest. Suddenly, he _______ a vineyard, full of _______ . The fox was ________. "Ah, I shall have a ______ breakfast!" he thought, entering the vineyard.

Circle the correct spelling:

1) (a) through (b) thruogh
2) (a) braekfast (b) breakfast
3) (a) delihgted (b) delighted
4) (a) delicious (b) dilecious
5) (a) thought (b) thougt

Tick (✓) the correct option:

1) A fox was wandering

a) through the forest. ☐

b) through the town. ☐

2) He saw a

a) vineyard. ☐

b) orchard. ☐

3) The grapes were

a) hanging very high. ☐

b) kept on the ground. ☐

4) The fox

a) could not grab the grapes. ☐

b) ate the grapes. ☐

5) They look

a) sweet. ☐

b) sour anyway. ☐

JANE AND HER PUPPY

Everyone liked Jane, because she was always pleasant and cheerful. One day, when Jane was coming home from school, she saw a small puppy lying on the side of the road. It could not walk because its leg was hurt.

Jane gently picked up the puppy and took it home. Her mother tied a bandage on the puppy's leg and gave it some milk and cookies. It

was so happy, it looked at Jane and wagged its tail. Jane told the puppy, "You can always stay with me, little puppy!"

Fill in the blanks:

1) Everyone ______________ Jane.

2) She was always __________ and cheerful.

3) One day, Jane was coming home from ________________.

4) She saw a small _________ lying on the side of the _______________.

5) The puppy's leg was _____________.

6) Jane gently _____________ up the puppy.

7) Her mother tied a ______________ on the puppy's leg.

8) The puppy _______ at Jane and _________ its tail.

ASKING QUESTIONS

How old are you?
I am five years old.

How do you go to school?
I go to school by bus.

What is your favourite food?
My favourite food is noodles.

What time do you go to bed?

I go to bed at eight o'clock.

Circle the correct spelling:

1) (a) yaers (b) years

2) (a) scoohl (b) school

3) (a) favourite (b) favuorite

4) (a) noodels (b) noodles

5) (a) waht (b) what

6) (a) time (b) tiem

7) (a) eihgt (b) eight

DING, DONG, BELL

Ding, dong bell,
Pussy's in the well,
Who put her in?
Little Tommy thin.
Who pulled her out?
Little Tommy stout.

Write 'RIGHT' or 'WRONG' in the boxes:

1) The bell rings 'ding dong'. [ ]

2) The pussy is in the river. [ ]

3) Little Tommy thin put the pussy in the well. [ ]

4) Little Tommy stout did not pull the pussy out. [ ]

Match the pictures with the text:

1) 

2) 

3) 

a) Who put her in? Little Tommy thin.

b) Who pulled her out? Little Tommy stout.

c) Pussy's in the well.

THE WHEELS ON THE BUS

The wheels on the bus
go round and round,
Round and round,
round and round.
The wheels on the bus
go round and round,
All day long.
The people on the bus
go up and down,
Up and down, up and down.
The people on the bus

go up and down,
All day long.
The doors on the bus
go open and shut,
Open and shut, open and shut.
The doors on the bus
go open and shut,
All day long.

Complete the sentences:

1) The wheels on the bus go ______________
__________________________________.

2) The people on the bus go ______________
___________________________.

3) The doors on the bus go _______________
_________________________.

4) The ____________________________________ go
round and round.

5) The ____________________________________ go
up and down.

Label the pictures choosing the words from the triangle:

shut wheel

open

______

______

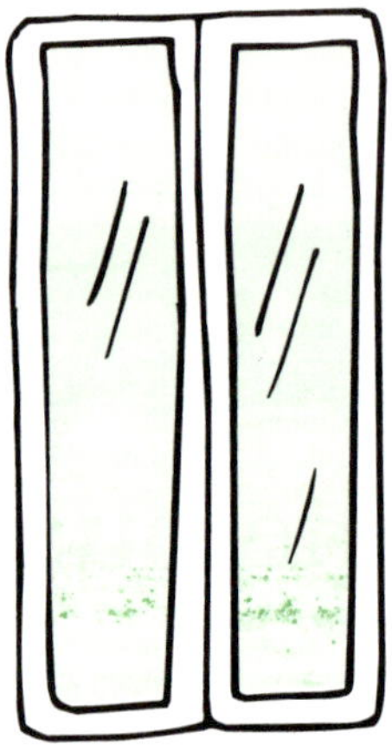

______

Circle the correct spelling:

1) (a) wheals (b) wheels

2) (a) round (b) ruond

3) (a) peaple (b) people

4) (a) shut (b) shat

5) (a) opan (b) open

DOING ACTIONS - 2

Sally is **washing** the clothes.

Peter is **riding** a bicycle.

John is **driving** a car.

The cat is **chasing** a rat.

George is **watering** the plants.

The grocer is **selling** rice.

Henry is **climbing** the steps.

I am **reading** the newspaper.

Choose the correct word from the box and fill in the blanks:

Reading	**Washing**	**Driving**
Climbing	**Riding**	
Watering	**Chasing**	**Selling**

1) Henry is _______________ the steps.

2) George is ________________ the plants.

3) Sally is _______________ the clothes.

4) The grocer is ______________ rice.

5) Peter is ___________ a bicycle.

6) The cat is ___________ a rat.

Circle the 'Verbs' (action words):

1) I am reading the newspaper.

2) John is driving a car.

3) George is watering the plants.

4) Henry is climbing the steps.

MY VISIT TO THE SEASIDE

Last week, my father took us to the seaside. My sister and I played in the sand and made sand-castles.

We were delighted to see the seashells, crabs and shining pebbles. We collected seashells. We clapped our hands when the waves wet our legs. We also saw a boat in the distance. My father bought us ice-cream.

Match the following:

1) The waves	a) ice-cream
2) We played	b) our hands
3) We collected	c) wet our legs
4) We clapped	d) in the sand
5) My father bought	e) seashells

Tick (✓) the correct option:

1. My father took us to the

a) seaside ☐

b) village ☐

2. My sister and I

a) played ☐

b) slept ☐

3. We saw a

a) car in the distance ☐

b) boat in the distance ☐

THE RAINY SEASON

My favourite season is the rainy season. I am very happy when it rains. I like to play in the water. My sister and I make paper boats and float them in the water.

I make small boats and my sister makes big boats. We wear our raincoats and enjoy wading through water.

Match the following:

1) We make	a) when it rains
2) I am very happy	b) raincoats
3) We enjoy	c) is the rainy season
4) My sister makes	d) paper boats
5) My favourite season	e) wading through water
6) We wear our	f) big boats

Fill in the blanks:

1) My favourite season is the ______ season.

2) I am very ________ when it rains.

3) I like to play in the __________.

4) My sister and I make _________ boats.

5) We wear our _____________.

THE LION AND THE MOUSE

One day, while a lion was sleeping in his den, a small mouse ran over his face. The lion caught the mouse and was about to kill it. The mouse said, "Please do not kill me. One day, I may be able to help you." The lion took pity on the mouse and let him go.

After a few days, a hunter caught the lion in his net. The lion roared loudly. The mouse heard the roar and ran to help the lion. He cut the

net with his sharp teeth and set the lion free. The lion thanked the mouse for saving his life.

Write 'RIGHT' or 'WRONG' in the boxes:

1) One day, a lion was sleeping in his den. [ ]

2) A very big mouse ran over the lion's face. [ ]

3) The lion could not catch the mouse. [ ]

4) A hunter caught the lion in his net. [ ]

5) The mouse heard the roar but did not help the lion. [ ]

6) The lion thanked the mouse for saving his life. [ ]

HOMES OF ANIMALS

A rabbit lives
in a **burrow**.

A bear lives
in a **cave**.

A rat lives
in a **hole**.

A fish lives in **water**.

A bird lives in a **nest**.

A dog lives in a **kennel**.

A lion lives
in a **den**.

A horse lives
in a **stable**.

A cow lives
in a **shed**.

Write True (T) or False (F):

1) A dog lives in a burrow. ( )

2) A fish lives in water. ( )

3) A rat lives in a den. ( )

4) A bear lives in a cave. ( )

5) A rabbit lives in a stable. ( )

6) A cow lives in a kennel. ( )

7) A bird lives in a nest. ( )

8) A lion does not live in a den. ( )

Match the animals with their homes:

1) Bear	a) Den
2) Fish	b) Stable
3) Rabbit	c) Kennel
4) Lion	d) Nest
5) Rat	e) Burrow
6) Horse	f) Water
7) Dog	g) Shed
8) Cow	h) Cave
9) Bird	i) Hole

Rearrange the jumbled letters and write the words correctly:

1) bitrab

____

2) sbleta

____

3) hrseo

____

4) rowbur

____

5) wtera

____

6) nelken

____

ANSWERS

Page 5
Rearrange the jumbled letters:
1) name 2) father 3) home 4) Rocky 5) barks 6) very 7) intelligent 8) strangers

Page 7
Choose the correct word from the box and fill in the blanks:
1) throwing 2) holding 3) carrying 4) drinking 5) lighting 6) chopping

Circle the 'Proper Nouns':
1) Mary 2) Jack 3) Lucy 4) Tara

Page 9
Strike out (✗) the incorrect option:
1) a 2) a 3) b 4) a

Choose the correct letters and complete the words:
1) le 2) up 3) ir 4) er 5) er 6) ck 7) ed 8) ay

Page 11
Write True (T) or False (F):
1) F 2) T 3) T 4) F 5) F 6) T

Rearrange the jumbled words and write the sentences correctly:
1) I eat with my mouth. 2) I see with my eyes. 3) I walk with my legs.
4) I clap with my hands. 5) I hear with my ears.

Page 13
Fill in the blanks:
1) sitting 2) eating 3) jackal, wanted 4) beautiful 5) crow 6) mouth
7) fell 8) away

Page 15
Complete the sentences:
1) pretty, doll 2) Lucy 3) beautiful 4) eyes, black
5) down, closes 6) sleep, next 7) favourite

Circle the correct spelling:
1) b 2) a 3) b 4) a 5) b

Page 17
Strike out (✗) the incorrect option:
1) b 2) a 3) a 4) b

Page 19
Fill in the blanks:
1) carrots 2) tiger's 3) burrow 4) carried 5) out 6) cry

Page 20
Tick (✓) the correct option:
1) b 2) b

Page 21
3) c 4) c

Page 23
Choose the correct option and fill in the blanks:
1) sat 2) pie 3) thumb 4) plum 5) boy

Page 25
Colour the correct option:
1) Doctor 2) Nurses 3) Evening

Page 27
Write True (T) or False (F):
1) F 2) T 3) F 4) T 5) F 6) F 7) T

Page 29
Choose the correct word from the box and fill in the blanks:
1) to school 2) tasty food 3) nice stories 4) studies 5) candy, ice-cream

Label the pictures choosing the words from the triangle:

Food

candies

storybooks

Page 31
Fill in the blanks:
1) dove, ant 2) helped 3) hunter 4) pain 5) bit 6) away 7) thanked

Page 33
Write 'RIGHT' or' WRONG 'in the boxes:
1) RIGHT 2) WRONG 3) RIGHT 4) WRONG 5) WRONG

Choose the correct letters and complete the words:
1) last 2) gave 3) inside 4) enjoyed 5) trunk 6) monkey

Page 35
Match the following:
1) e 2) f 3) d 4) b 5) c 6)g 7) a

Page 37
Write True (T) or False (F):
1) (F) 2) (F) 3) (T) 4) (F) 5) (T) 6) (F) 7) (T)

Rearrange the jumbled letters and write the words correctly:
1) beautiful 2) morning 3) garden 4) flowers 5) butterflies 6) plants

Page 39
Fill in the blanks:
1) friends 2) bicycle 3) baked 4) played 5) 'Happy Birthday' 6) kept

Page 40
Match them up:
Doctor - Nurse
Nest - Bird
Table - Chair

Page 41
Match them up:
Teacher - Blackboard
Bread - Jam
Racket - Ball

Page 42
Choose the correct letter from the bracket to complete the word:
1) Bread 2) Nest 3) Rain 4) Nurse 5) Table 6) Clouds

Page 45
Write True (T) or False (F):
1) (F) 2) (F) 3) (T) 4) (F) 5) (T) 6) (F) 7) (T) 8) (T)

Page 47
Fill in the blanks:
1) little 2) fleece 3) went 4) lamb, go

Match the following:
1) c 2) d 3) b 4) a

Page 49
Match the animals with the sounds:
1) e 2) f 3) b 4) c 5) a 6) d

Page 51
Match the following:
1) c 2) a 3) b 4) f 5) d 6) e

Label the pictures choosing the words from the box:

Doll

My father

My sister

Car

Page 53
Arrange the sentences in the correct order:
1) (4) 2) (2) 3) (1) 4) (3) 5) (5) 6) (8) 7) (7) 8) (6)

Page 54
Match the pictures with the text:

c) And one for the little boy, who lives down the lane.

d) Yes sir! Yes sir! Three bags full.

b) Baa, baa, black sheep, have you any wool?

a) One for my master, one for my dame.

Page 56
Complete the paragraph:
hungry, saw, juicy, delighted, delicious

Circle the correct spelling:
1) (a) 2) (b) 3) (b) 4) (a) 5) (a)

Page 57
Tick (✓) the correct option:
1) a 2) a 3) a 4) a 5) b

Page 59
Fill in the blanks:
1) liked 2) pleasant 3) school 4) puppy, road 5) hurt 6) picked 7) bandage
8) looked, wagged

Page 61
Circle the correct spelling
1) b 2)b 3) a 4) b 5) b 6) a 7) b

Page 63
Write 'RIGHT' or 'WRONG' in the boxes:
1) RIGHT 2) WRONG 3) RIGHT 4) WRONG

Match the pictures with the text:

c) Pussy's in the well.

a) Who put her in? Little Tommy thin.

b) Who pulled her out? Little Tommy stout.

Page 65

Complete the sentences

1) round and round 2) up and down 3) open and shut 4) the wheels on the bus 5) the people on the bus

Page 66

Label the pictures choosing the words from the triangle:

wheel

open

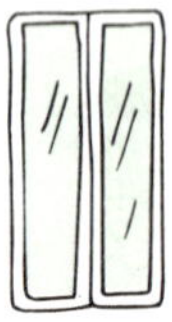

shut

Circle the correct spelling:

1) b 2) a 3) b 4) a 5) b

Page 69

Choose the correct word from the box and fill in the blanks:

1) climbing 2) watering 3) washing 4) selling 5) driving 6) chasing

Circle the 'Verbs' (action words):

1) reading 2) driving 3) watering 4) climbing

Page 71

Match the following:

1) c 2) d 3) e 4) b 5) a

Tick (✓) the correct option:

1) seaside 2) played 3) boat in the distance

Page 73

Match the following:

1) d 2) a 3) e 4) f 5) c 6) b

Fill in the blanks:

1) rainy 2) happy 3) water 4) paper 5) raincoats

Page 75

Write 'RIGHT' or 'WRONG' in the boxes:

1) RIGHT 2) WRONG 3) WRONG 4) RIGHT 5) WRONG 6) RIGHT

Page 79

Write True (T) or False (F):

1) (F) 2) (T) 3) (F) 4) (T) 5) (F) 6) (F) 7) (T) 8) (F)

Page 80

Match the animals with their homes:

1) h 2) f 3) e 4) a 5) i 6) b 7) c 8) g 9) d